EXAMINE FIRST, YOURSELF

A TESTAMENT TO SPIRITUAL ACCOUNTABILITY, SELF-REFLECTION AND UNDERSTANDING.

ANGELA CRUDUPT

Angela Crudupt

Examine First, Yourself: A Testament to Spiritual Accountability,
Self-Reflection and Understanding
Copyright © 2017 by Angela Crudupt, Sent by Jesus, LLC.
Visit the author's website at www.AngelaCrudupt.com
Follow on Instagram @angelacrudupt

Edited by: Amanda Pittman and Erick Markley
Formatted by: PublishMate
Cover Design: Angela Crudupt
Headshot: William Johnson

For information regarding special discounts for bulk purchase, please email
us at info@AngelaCrudupt.com

Dedication

My Beloved LORD and Savior, Jesus Christ: Thank You for being Faithful when I have been faithless. Thank You, Jesus for Your grace, mercy, and compassion. Most of all, thank You for the gift of repentance! I live to worship and serve You.

Erick Markley, thank you for challenging me to always be a doer of the Word and not a hearer only.

Table of Contents

Introduction

————————•————————

Chosen for Something Different

"For this reason I bow my knees to the Father of our Lord Jesus Christ, from whom the whole family in heaven and earth is named, that He would grant you, according to the riches of His glory, to be strengthened with might through His Spirit in the inner man, that Christ may dwell in your hearts through faith; that you, being rooted and grounded in love, may be able to comprehend with all the saints what is the width and length and depth and height to know the love of Christ which passes knowledge; that you may be filled with the fullness of God"
(Ephesians 3:14-19).

In serving as a minister in the local church as well as in the community, one of the most difficult assignments I must submit to is giving a Word of chastisement. Many believers desire to hear prophecies of prosperity, joy, increase, favor, and abundance. Most Christians carry out their walk from the place of need; they look to God as nothing more than a Provider. And, though God can most certainly bring our desires to pass, that is not my ministry. I've been called, through Christ Jesus, to guide the people of God under

His subjection. I am often called to issue messages of rebuke and alignment. Therefore, I preach and proclaim the Spirit of forgiveness, self-control, faithfulness, prayer, repentance, service, purity, longsuffering, love, submission, generosity, faith, and obedience.

At times, my spirit is grieved. I weep and mourn for the people of God who are seeking, needing, or desiring restoration, opportunities, miracles, and freedom, yet they refuse to surrender their soul; they refuse to surrender their heart; they refuse to surrender their possessions; they refuse to surrender their pride, and they refuse to surrender their doubt for unwavering faith!

It is difficult enough for me to be chastised daily by the Holy Spirit for my own struggles and shortcomings, but on top of that, I have been assigned to sternly call the sons and daughters of Jesus back to Him—a privilege and an honor that I am not worthy of by any standard, and I am consistently thankful for! However, what I've come to learn is that this walk at times is *lonely* for those who have been called; people don't want to hear the unadulterated Gospel—they want to hear a selective, watered-down gospel. They want to hear that they're blessed going in and blessed coming out; they want to hear they're the head and not the tail, above and not beneath; they want to hear, "you're healed, go your way." They *don't* want to hear, "repent, for the Kingdom of God is at hand" (Matthew 3:2); they don't want to hear "feed the poor" (Matthew 25:35-40); they don't want to hear, "deny yourself, pick up your cross and follow Jesus" (Matthew 16:24); they don't want to hear, "those who desire to be great, let him first be the slave" (Mark10:34); and they don't want to hear, "bless those who curse you" (Luke 6:26).

Many of you have been called for an extraordinary assignment in ministry. Take courage in knowing this: He who hears you hears Me saith the Lord, he who rejects you rejects Me, and he who rejects Me rejects Him who sent Me (Luke 10:16).

Prayer

O LORD, hear the cry of Your servant and touch the hearts, souls, and minds of Your people. Give them the strength to endure temptation and the confidence to overcome rejection. Encourage Your people to live holy lives, to honor You in word and deed, and to bring You glory in all that they do. In Jesus' name I pray!

Beloved, you have been *anointed to suffer.*

Everyone has a divine purpose; my hope is that through the power of Jesus Christ, you walk boldly in yours!

With Love,

Minister Angela

Remember, Christ died for you! Trust Him!

Angela Crudupt

Chapter 1

———————•———————

Women in the Church

"There is neither Jew nor Greek, there is neither bond nor free, there is neither male nor female: for ye are all one in Christ Jesus"
(Galatians 3:28).

Women, receive and be accountable to who the spirit of the LORD has called you to be! Most women treat their divine call so casually. Oftentimes, waiting for a man to validate their Kingdom assignment. In our spiritual communities, we regularly and respectfully address men by their title and last name, while frequently calling women who have been chosen in a similar capacity by their first name, even their nicknames. I've witnessed firsthand men who simply come to church in a suit be addressed with the esteemed title of "reverend" or "doctor," while a woman who has the anointing to make demons tremble and flee, or who preaches with power and authority of the Holy Ghost be addressed as, "hey girl," or repeatedly, by their first name. I have witnessed men get ordained that struggle finding the book of Saint John, or are unable to teach a Sunday school lesson with a teacher guide in their hand with a 2 months advance notice. And, my God, I have watched women humbly, submissively, and constantly surrender their lives to follow Jesus, yet to be told they have to wait until their babies turn 13, serve for 33 years (the age of Jesus), or must serve in every auxiliary of the church for an extended period of time before being ordained.

My intention is not to stir up any arrogant or rebellious spirit. Women, in the most humble manner possible, receive and be accountable to your Christ-given assignment. It doesn't matter what people address me as, I know who God called me to be! And, I refuse to settle for sexist standards in the church. Not only do I value the virtue of submission, but I also submit to it. If you call me "Angela," with all humility and grace, I respond. And, if you call me "minister," with all humility and grace, I respond. I thank God that my mother had a discerning spirit when I was in her womb by naming me Angela, which derives from the Greek word Angelos and because of her obedience, I am reminded that I am a messenger from God. I'm not perfect, but I'm discerning and have been chosen. Because I know God appointed me in a ministerial capacity, I am consistently disciplining myself to align with that of a minister.

Beloved daughters of Christ, many of you are more than simply a "woman of God," or, "sister so-and-so." Some of you have been called by God to be a prophetess, an evangelist, a missionary, a minister, a prayer warrior, a teacher of scripture and more. The bible says in Acts 2:17, "And it shall come to pass in the last days, that I (God) will pour out my Spirit upon all flesh: and your sons and your daughter shall prophesy (KJV)." Additionally, Galatians 3:28 proclaims, "There is neither Jew nor Gentile, neither slave nor free, nor is there male and female, for you are all one in Christ Jesus (KJV)." If we are all one in Christ Jesus, and the Holy Spirit endowed us with different gifts to edify the church, surely they are important to hearken to.

Know who you are and don't allow *anyone* to reduce who Jesus has created you to be before the foundation of the world! Be humble, be loving, be gracious, be generous and be accountable to who the spirit of the LORD has called you to be!

Prayer

Dear Spirit of the Living God, encourage Your women! I beg of Thee! Remind them that you have given them power and authority to trample over scorpions and serpents and nothing by any means shall harm them. In Jesus name I pray!

Chapter 2

————•————

Fornication and Sexual Immorality —the Church's Responsibility

"Therefore we also, since we are surrounded by so great a cloud of witnesses, let us lay aside every weight, and the sin which so easily ensnares us, and let us run with endurance the race that is set before us, looking unto Jesus, the author and finisher of our faith,

who for the joy that was set before Him endured the cross, despising the shame, and has sat down at the right hand of the throne of God, our Father" (Hebrews 12:1-2).

Ironically, in a culture consumed with lust, pride, and greed, the Church is being viciously attacked for inadequately supporting those who are struggling with sexual immorality, especially, fornication. After continually witnessing the dialogue indicting the Church, as a minister of the Gospel and an imperfect woman, the Lord has called me to speak against such erroneous criticism.

First, the Church is the bride of Christ, as flawed as she may have become in some communities, she was never called to replace the unadulterated Word of God. Therefore, the baseline premise of the Church is and always will be holiness: "having been built on the foundation of the apostles and prophets, Jesus Christ Himself being the chief cornerstone, in whom the whole building, being fitted together, grows into a holy temple in the Lord, in whom you also are being built together for a dwelling place of God in the Spirit" (Ephesians 2:20-22). 1 Peter 1:16 simply states, "You shall be holy, for I (Jesus) am holy."

To a degree, it may be somewhat accurate to suggest that the Church could do a little more; however, to hold the Church accountable for not being responsive or useful in their approach is misrepresentation at best. The root cause of the issue of sexual immorality is consistently wildly overlooked and repeatedly unaddressed which is **individual accountability**.

Few want to acknowledge that they are struggling with sexual immorality because they are indulging in pornography.

Few want to acknowledge that they are struggling with sexual immorality because they take pleasure in watching crude movies.

Few want to acknowledge that they are struggling with fornication or adultery because they listen to music that degrades and/or sexualizes women, planting seeds of lustful desire or demeaning behavior within them.

Few want to acknowledge that they are struggling with fornication, adultery, masturbation or sexual sins because they're searching for #relationshipgoals on Instagram or Facebook, allowing social media to plant seeds of confusion in their minds about how they ought to handle conflict or pursue relationships.

Few want to acknowledge that they are struggling with fornication, adultery, masturbation or other sexual sins because they idolize and follow half-naked celebrities on the social platforms.

Few want to acknowledge that they are struggling with sexual immorality because they go to secular clubs, bars, or concerts that expose their spirit to scantily clad women, spiritually-undisciplined men, and lust-filled lyrics, most which are demonic in nature.

Few want to acknowledge that they are struggling with fornication because they lay up in a bed with a person that is not their spouse until the early morning.

There is your honest dialogue! The issue is not the Church, but individual **compromise**. Many believers compromise their spiritual integrity and then want everyone to compromise with them. **No, crucify your flesh!** We must be holy for the LORD our God is holy (1 Peter 1:16). Stop expecting the Church to continually and repeatedly teach and give attention to area's where you are exercising absolutely no self-discipline. The LORD says it this way, "If My people who are called by My name will humble themselves, and pray and seek My face, and turn from their wicked ways, then I will hear from heaven, and will forgive their sin and heal their land" (2 Chronicles 7:14).

Learn how to handle adversity; learn how to suffer; learn what it means to deny yourself; take up your cross and follow God. Proverbs 4:7 (KJV) says, "wisdom is the principal thing; therefore get wisdom: and with all thy getting get understanding." Be accountable! Take captive every vain imagination and make it obedient to Christ (2 Corinthian 2:5).

Jesus never promised the path of salvation to be painless or comfortable. "Narrow is the way; for wide is the gate and broad is the way that leads to destruction, and there are many who go in by it. Because narrow is the gate and difficult is the way which leads to life and there are few who find it" (Matthew 7:13-14). What Jesus did **promise is a yoke and a burden**, which is easy and light **ONLY** in Him (Matthew 11:28-30).

This is why marriages are falling apart; this is why abortion clinics stay in business; this is why people are sexually abusing children; this is why there are so many pregnancy's outside of marriage; this is why our society is consumed with sexual immorality—because of compromise.

Fornication and Sexual Immorality—the Church Responsibility

Having the mind of Jesus, the Church was created to preach the Gospel to the poor, proclaim deliverance to the captives, recover sight to the (spiritually) blind, release the oppressed, heal the sick, raise the (spiritually) dead, cleanse the lepers, drive out demons, call sinners to repentance, provide for the poor, the needy, the orphaned, and the widowed (Luke 4:18, Luke 5:32, and, Luke 10:9). And, unbelievers and undisciplined Christians are wanting the Church to compromise the Word of God. But, the bible boldly announced that God is the same yesterday, today and forevermore (Hebrews 13:8). Therefore, regardless of the struggle in our flesh, His standard will not change, His Word is good enough, and His convicting Spirit is good enough. Neither holiness nor love must ever be compromised! Regardless of the struggles of unstable humans.

Thus says the LORD, "As many as I love, I rebuke and chasten. Therefore be zealous and repent" (Revelation 3:19).

Purify yourself by allowing the Holy Spirit to cleanse, restore and renew your very soul. "No longer be conformed to this world, but be transformed by the renewing of your mind, that you may prove (some translations use the word 'test') what is that good and acceptable perfect will of God" (Romans 12:2 KJV). Stop asking the Church to compromise with the desires of your flesh!

Additionally, if you're attending a church that is compromising the integrity of God, you should be the example of God's purity by being loving and holy, continually abiding in the spirit of repentance and faithfulness.

And, it is not that prayer is not good enough, it is that we don't believe in the Power of the Living God whom we are called to pray to. It is not that prayer is not good enough, it is that too many people expect their prayers to be answered, even when outside the will of God. This is not biblical. The bible says, "If you abide in Me, and My words abide in you, you will ask what you desire, and it shall be done for you" (John 15:7). **"Abide" means to act in accordance with; to endure without yielding; to accept without objection; to bear, to suffer.** Another words, "Put on the whole armour of God, that ye may be able to stand against the wiles of the devil" (Ephesians 6:11 KJV).

It is not that prayer does not work, it is that we don't believe in the power of prayer and fasting, or the power of wise counsel. **Even with all that, we are called to suffer... furthermore, you have been anointed to suffer!**

Fornication, adultery, masturbation or any other area of sexual immorality is never the Holy-Spirit-filled Church's fault; it is never the pastor's, minister's, deacon's or teacher's fault; it is never the leadership's fault (unless you were molested or abused in the church). **The problem for the overwhelming**

majority of the body of Christ is that there is no accountability. The Bible says you are *accountable to God (Romans 14:12).* **It is not someone else's responsibility to crucify our flesh.** We must hold ourselves accountable. The act of fornication, adultery as well as other sexual sins are an issue of lust, lack of self-control, and **lack of accountability to God.**

The pastor is not your God; the minister is not your God; the deacon is not your God; the church leadership is not your God. At best, they are called to be an example of Christ-like character. **Stop expecting the people in the Church to make provision for what the blood of Christ already did.** If you are struggling with sexual immorality, I strongly recommend you exercise the following:

1. Repent Frequently – ask Jesus to purify your spirit and heed His promptings; pray without ceasing (Acts 3:19, 2 Peter 3:9).

2. Study the word of God – Remember, Jesus is your God. Invest in your relationship with Him (2 Timothy 2:15, Acts 17:11)!

3. Strengthen your relationship with God – Pass those test (2 Corinthians 13:15).

4. Serve those less fortunate; take the focus of yourself – In and outside the church (Matthew 25:34-46).

5. Exercise the virtue of longsuffering – Be discipline. Don't put yourself in compromising positions (James 4:7, Romans 2:4).

6. Separate yourself from secular influences (1 Corinthians 6:9, 2 Timothy 3:5).

7. Seek and connect with wise counsel (Proverbs 11:14, Proverbs 15:22).

8. Form relationships with spirit-filled believers who honor their bodies and believe in purity (Proverbs 24:6).

The Bible tells us in 1 Corinthians 6:18 to "flee sexual immorality." **Do not** entertain, do not compromise, do not indulge, **but flee!** The Holman Christian Standard bible uses the phrase, "Run from sexual immorality!" And, the International Standard Version translates as "Keep on running away from sexual immorality!" I am reminded of Colossians 3:5, "Put to death, therefore, the components of your earthly nature: sexual immorality, impurity, lust, evil desires, and greed which is idolatry." And, 1 Thessalonians 4:3, "For it is God's will that you should be holy: You must abstain from sexual immorality."

Dear beloved brothers and sisters in Christ, this is the type of language the Church is called to use. The Church is called to rebuke, bind, cast down, pray against—NOT coddle, pamper, negotiate or compromise with—the lust of the flesh.

Fornication and Sexual Immorality—the Church Responsibility

Sexual immorality is exceedingly **dangerous**. Sexual Immorality (fornication, adultery, etc.) makes us susceptible to AIDS, HIV, Herpes, and other sexually transmitted infections. It dismantles marriages, it breaks up homes, it distracts people from their purpose, it increases the risk of unplanned pregnancies, it builds anger and resentment, it hinders relationships, and most importantly, it separates us from the spirit of Christ. This separation not only weakens our ability to discern spiritual truth, but also weakens our ability to fight against demonic influences.

Like many of you (saved and unsaved), I, too, previously suffered from many issues due to my undisciplined spirit. I exposed myself to demonic influences that seemed harmless on the surface. This included certain forms of entertainment, dressing in revealing attire, and hanging around people who had a form of godliness yet denied the power thereof. Fornication caused me an overwhelming amount of pain, grief, abuse, and heartache, which could have been easily avoided. I've found in my personal and professional relationships as well as serving in ministry that greed, pride, grief, addiction, self-loathing, rebellion, hate, jealously, heartache, distraction from purpose, and certain degrees of abuse are **always** connected to those who are engaging in some form of sexual immorality. **This confirms not only what the Word of God says, but what the Holy Spirit reveals.**

If you attend a church that remedies sexual immorality using the New Testament teachings, anointing oil, prayer meetings, fasting, and testimony sharing, consider yourself in good company! **Ask the LORD to help you with the rest, namely, self-discipline.**

The grace in Jesus Christ is sufficient – sufficient to forgive you, sufficient to love you, sufficient to guide you, sufficient to humble you, sufficient to purify you, sufficient to sustain you, and sufficient to forgive you again. Seek Him while He may be found.

"Blessed are those who hunger and thirst for righteousness, for they shall be filled" (Matthew 5:6).

Prayer

Dear Heavenly Father, Perfect and Faithful One; purify the soul of not only the fornicator, adulterer, or the sexually immoral, but cleanse also those who by their artistry, career choice, or behavior, lead others into bondage. In Jesus' name I pray!

Chapter 3

————•————

Sharing

In John 13:34 Jesus said, "A new commandment I give to you, that you love one another: **just as I have loved you, you also are to love one another.** By this all people will know that you are **My disciples**, if you have love for one another." One of the greatest desires God has for us is that our love be expressed through meeting the needs of each other by sincerely, wholeheartedly, and continually abounding in generosity: giving of ourselves and giving of our resources, being a reflection of the Jesus, who has met our every need.

Whenever believers give and receive in the Spirit of love, they grow closer together, and the body of Christ flourishes as noted in Acts 4:34-35 which reads, "Neither was there any among them that lacked: for as many as were possessors of lands or houses sold them, and brought the prices of the things that were sold, and laid them down at the apostles' feet: and distribution was made unto every man according as he had need."

What makes Acts 4:34-35 particularly significant is that it was recorded during the establishment of the Church.

Early believers provided regularly for the financial support of one another, **especially those who experienced lack.** The early church recognized that it had a responsibility to care for those in need and they showed their commitment to each other in radical ways. Many sold their houses and lands and took the proceeds to the Apostles who then distributed it to those in *need*.

The church flourished because the Spirit of God within the people flourished. What was exceptionally unique was that the selling of property and the donating of goods was **completely volunteer**.

This practice of support, compassion, and generosity is not a New Testament ideal or alternative, but a biblical principal. Additionally, it is not exclusive to an individual. In Exodus 36:2-7, Moses called on the children of Israel, along with gifted artisans who had the heart of the LORD to support in making the sanctuary. The Bible said, "So they continued bringing him freewill offerings every morning." There was no need for continual commission or follow-up, for it was a free will offering and the Israelites gave liberally. Additionally, they brought their offerings every morning, which displayed their commitment as well as their sense of urgency. It is noted that there was such an abundance in giving, that Moses had to command and *restrain* the people from bringing, for the material they had was sufficient for all the work to be done (Exodus 36:4-7).

The Spirit of the early New Testament church was "of one heart and of one soul." And, that one heart and one soul was unified with Jesus Christ. Interestingly, donors weren't concerned with who the beneficiaries of their extreme generosity, they gave simply from the outpouring of their heart.

In Matthew 25:35-46, Jesus Himself reveals to us the heart a believer should seek, another example of giving: He said, *"for I was hungry and you gave Me food; I was thirsty and you gave Me drink; I was a stranger and you took Me in; I was naked and you clothed Me; I was sick and you visited Me; I was in prison and you came to Me.'*

"Then the righteous will answer Him, saying, 'Lord, when did we see You hungry and feed You, or thirsty and give You drink? When did we see You a stranger and take You in, or naked and clothe You? Or when did we see You sick, or in prison, and come to You?' And the King will answer and say to them, 'Assuredly, I say to you, inasmuch as you did it to one of the least of these My brethren, you did it to Me.'

"Then He will also say to those on the left hand, 'Depart from Me, you cursed, into the everlasting fire prepared for the devil and his angels: for I was hungry and you gave Me no food; I was thirsty and you gave Me no drink; I was a stranger and you did not take Me in, naked and you did not clothe Me, sick and in prison and you did not visit Me.'

"Then they also will answer Him, saying, 'Lord, when did we see You hungry or thirsty or a stranger or naked or sick or in prison, and did not minister to You?' Then He will answer them, saying,

'Assuredly, I say to you, inasmuch as you did not do it to one of the least of these, you did not do it to Me."

The scripture above highlights perfectly the heart of Jesus as it relates to sharing, giving and caring for those in need.

C.L. Lewis, Christian novelist, poet, academic, and theologian presents the following statement which properly denotes the heart of the early church; he says, "Only a real risk tests the reality of a belief."

Giving looks different for everyone, as God leads us differently in serving each other and the church. However, I pose a question that simply requires your private thoughts: what are you willing to risk for the body of Christ as an act of obedience to resemble Jesus in giving?

The early believers weren't concerned with comfort, they were committed to a commission—the Great Commission.

Prayer

Dear Father God, continue to prune our heart so that it may resemble the love and compassion found in You. Heavenly Father, open up opportunities for us to serve each other and reflect the obedient Spirit found in You. Separate us from greed and pride. Help us, O Jesus, to give more openly and to deny ourselves so that we may inherit eternal life.

O Jesus, I pray that this chapter brings forth clarity and assists in building Your Kingdom. In Jesus' name I pray.

Chapter 4

———————•———————

Know Your Name

"Paul, a bondservant ("bondservant" is translated as "slave") of God and an apostle of Jesus Christ, according to the faith of God's elect and the acknowledgment of the truth which accords with godliness" (Titus 1:1-1).

Out of the 27 books in the New Testament, Apostle Paul's authorship is attributed to approximately half. Apostle Paul, a prolific and eloquent scholar of the Old Testament, "circumcised the eighth day, of the stock of Israel, of the tribe of Benjamin, a Hebrew of the Hebrews; concerning the law, a Pharisee... concerning the righteousness which is in the law, blameless" proclaimed, **"what things were gain to me, these I have counted loss for Christ. I have suffered the loss of all things, and count them as rubbish, that I may gain Christ and being found in Him"** (Philippians 3:5-8).

Paul, the ascribed author to 13 of the New Testament books, considered his astonishing and impressive achievements as a Pharisee to be insignificant compared to what he was called to do in Christ—proclaim the gospel of Jesus Christ and Him crucified. **The most honored and respected role which Apostle Paul esteemed over every other facet of his life was discipleship: being a disciplined follower of Jesus Christ.**

He honored his calling with such personal accountability that 10 out of the roughly 13 letters written by Paul, he promptly and systematically asserted himself as an Apostle prior to addressing his audience. In fact, almost all the New Testament writers introduced themselves with such **certainty of self-actualization – servant of Jesus Christ.** It was not that the Apostle Paul or any of the other New Testament writers were prideful in their calling, rather, it was quite the opposite. The disciples took pride in denying themselves for the work of the ministry.

There are so many secular names that believers submit or conform to that are completely separate from the will of God over their lives—names that degrade the character of who Christ created us to be.

As a minister of the gospel, I understand my role: to pray, preach, and teach. My assignment, therefore, is prioritized around giving myself continually to prayer and to the ministry of the Word (Acts 6:4). Though I love the local church and I love the people of God, I will not allow myself to be *consumed* with activities that are not tied to God's will over my life – in or out of the church. With that being said, God uses a template called "process." Process is a template of pruning and preparation to develop us for our purpose, either in this moment or the next. There were occasions when Jesus will for me was to assist in finding shelter for individuals, prepare administrative or legal documents for my pastor, and support elderly women with household chores. The will of God over my life at times has meant carrying the woman of God's belongings, and even cleaning the men's restroom in the church during a clean-up day. **There have been moments in my Christian journey as a minister in the local church when the will of God over my life was to sit; observe!**

Through much error, I have learned to **prayerfully** consider every assignment before moving forward—no matter how big or how small. I have humbly and respectfully turned down perceived esteemed leadership positions within the church because it had nothing to do with my purpose or, may pose as a distraction to it; similarly, I have declined several high-paying positions in the secular that would hinder my assignment. I have grown to know my name and trust that God is directing my path. In the same manner, as I continue to mature in Christ, I seek to continually align my behavior to that of a minister. It's deeper than just knowing your purpose; we must also submit to that call. There are places I no longer go, types of music I will no longer allow in my spirit, and people I will no longer associate with. And it is not easy, it is a grieving process of dying to myself daily; a daily pursuit of submitting to the "process" of being purified for the work of the ministry.

I have embraced my call while accepting how frail of a human being I am, made of mere dust. Jesus said: "Watch and pray so that you will not fall into temptation. The spirit is willing, but the flesh is weak" (Matthew 26:40). Because I have experienced so much destruction in my own life: abandonment, rape, abuse, depression, anxiety, manipulation, and unemployment to name a few, I understand how weak I truly am when separated from Jesus. Therefore, I earnestly guard my heart and assignment! Prayer is also essential in knowing your name (purpose) and embracing who God has called you to be. We must be sensitive to the prompting of the Holy Spirit. His thoughts are not like our thoughts neither are our ways His ways (Isaiah 55:8).

Almost two years prior to being called to serve in the ministry, Jesus called me to read the Bible regularly to elderly people at a convalescent home among other things. I had no idea that God was preparing me to teach and proclaim His gospel in the Church. Simply put, be available and do not overlook small beginnings—God may be preparing you for a divine assignment.

I once overheard a respected Pastor of mine share a piece of advice with a colleague of his that I will never forget. He said, **"You cannot be busy, you have to be goal-oriented. Mission objective: you have to be on-purpose!"** That statement has helped shape how I will forever operate in ministry as well as life. It is a constant reminder that our access into eternity will not be based on accomplishing our goals, completing tasks, or simply being busy, but our access into eternity will be based on submitting to the Father's will. In Matthew 7:21 Jesus said, "Not everyone who says to Me, 'Lord, Lord,' shall enter the kingdom of heaven, but he who does the will of My Father in heaven." Jesus continued, explaining how He will one day address those who were **busy but weren't purposeful**, "I never knew you; depart from me, you workers of lawlessness" (Matthew 7:23)!

Apostle Paul knew his assignment. He did not allow himself to become distracted, nor was he intimidated by his role in the body of Christ; though **by faith**, it took him 14 years to walk fully in his purpose, pressing through the stigma of being known as a "Christian" killer. Jesus can and will use ANYONE! Never allow your past to hinder your future!

Jesus has called many of you to a divine assignment in His kingdom: discipleship. It is a position of spiritual authority that can bring souls closer to Jesus, regardless of your past. But, you must be confident in your present and passionately pursue who God has ordained you to be before the foundation of the earth. In 1 Corinthians 9:27, the Apostle Paul said, "But I discipline my body and bring it into subjection, lest, when I have preached to others, I myself should become disqualified." While operating in your name (purpose), whether it is by being a spouse, parent, caretaker, teacher, developer, investor, non-profit organizer, minister, etc. be disciplined in your call.

Here are 3 practical ways to begin effectively walking in your call:

1. **Pray** – The Father takes pleasure in us seeking Him. It is though prayer that He directs and purifies us (Jeremiah 33:3, Matthew 6:6, Luke 11:9, Philippians 4:6).

2. **Submit** - Releasing control to Jesus not only develops humility, but it also opens up opportunity for God to use us. Yield, and apply the "Fruit of the Spirit" to every area of your life: home, work, interactions, etc. Additionally, as you seek to become more like Christ, partner with Jesus in purifying your spirit. We cannot commune with God and sin at the same time. (Read Proverbs 3:5-6, Matthew 6:33, John 15:7, Romans 12:1, 1 Peter 5:6)

3. **Obey** – Obedience is an invaluable virtue. The Bible says obedience is better than sacrifice – there is nothing more powerful that you can do to show Jesus that you reverence Him and that you're prepared to handle His purpose for your life than to obey Him in your current season! (Read Isiah 1:19, Matthew 25:23 Luke 16:10, John 14:15, Acts 5:29)

Prayer

Dear Heavenly Father, Faithful and Loving Savior and Spirit of Truth. O Jesus I pray that You separate us from every place that contradicts Your will. I pray, Master, that You separate us from every person who distracts us from Your purpose. O Abba Father, I pray that You separate us from every opportunity that doesn't glorify You. O Deliverer, bind us to the brokenhearted, bind us to the orphans; O Master, bind us to the fatherless so we may have the fortitude to share Your unfailing love. Break our flesh and cast down our pride so that through repentance and meekness in You we will continually abide.

Chapter 5

———•———

Liberty – Freedom through the Grace of God

"Now the LORD is the Spirit: and where the Spirit of the LORD is, there is liberty" (2 Corinthians 3:17).

In this particular Scripture above, the Apostle Paul refers to the freedom from psychological bondage. His premise in the Epistle of 2 Corinthians was that our mind not be corrupted from the simplicity in Christ; that our mental and emotional state be rooted in the glory that was revealed in Jesus, the hope our Savior brings; that we would live as we are called.

This liberty that the Apostle Paul speaks of is the freedom from fear, freedom from guilt, and freedom from the power of sin. This freedom gives us a **true confidence in the Word of God**.

The liberty that is in the Spirit of the Lord does not guarantee separation from physical affliction.

The liberty that is in the Spirit of the Lord does not warrant separation from oppression. The liberty that is in the Spirit of the Lord does not promise separation from discrimination.

The liberty that is in the Spirit of the Lord, does not guarantee separation from persecution.

In fact, 2 Timothy 3:12 professes, "All who have a *desire* to live godly in Christ Jesus will suffer persecution."

What the Spirit of the LORD *does* cultivate is freedom from psychological bondage within our circumstance. *Regardless* of what situation we find ourselves in, **through the Spirit of the LORD**, we have the power to either endure it or overcome it. And, **only prayer can discern which way Jesus is leading you**.

For example, if you're working a profession that you loathe, God may be using that circumstance to build your character, strengthen your temperament, or prepare you for greater responsibility in the next level of purpose. You find liberty in that place when you don't rely on your employees or supervisors to supply or fulfill what only God can: peace, joy, understanding, or contentment. You still show up early, you maintain the highest level of integrity and professionalism, you're gracious and kind, you're positive and uplifting—you work for man as unto the LORD, knowing that from the LORD you will receive the inheritance as your reward. You are serving the LORD (Colossians 3:23-24).

Another example is enduring unemployment. We exercise our liberty during a season of unemployment when we don't seek validation from a potential employer. Instead, continue to seek validation from Jesus. Pray about process and purpose; ask the LORD to sustain you. Instead of using free time to catch up on gossip-filled reality shows, become consumed with social media or indulge in secular activities, read the Bible and start declaring His favor over your life. Sharpen your skillset by reading educational books or taking classes in the area God has called you to. Instead of laying around, volunteer your time at a shelter, a human-trafficking organization, a hospital, a hospice center, a senior citizen complex, or a daycare center. Apply for a short-term internship or pray about starting a business that will positively impact other believers as well as those who are less fortunate than you. Don't just be busy, but be goal-oriented, be mission objective. Continue to seek employment opportunities knowing that what **God has for you is for you!** Be open, patient, long-suffering, and prayerful, allowing this process to strengthen your faith. The just live by faith (Hebrews 10:38). "Though it tarries, wait for it; because it will surely come, It will not tarry" (Habakkuk 2:3).

I've experienced rape, abandonment from my biological father, homelessness, unemployment, deception, as well as a verbally and physically abusive relationship. For years, some of those experiences had me so completely bound until I decided to submit to and accept liberty through faith in Jesus Christ. I had to stop feeling sorry for myself and realize that my past situations don't define me, Jesus defines me; He calls me a daughter made in His image! In Him, I am a new creature, an heir to the King! Even more powerful, as I matured, I learned that God *was allowing* my testimony to take root!

There are many examples I can give, but none of them will be as effective as reading the Word of God for yourself and allowing the Holy Spirit to guide you.

Additionally, never allow anyone to use scripture to keep you bound to physical or verbal abuse. This is why it is so important to hide the scripture in your heart; when you understand scripture, you cannot be deceived by false doctrine or scriptural abuse, hindering your gift of liberation.

In John 8:31 Jesus said, "If you abide in My word, you are My disciples indeed. And you shall know the truth, and the truth shall make you free." This freedom is the liberty the Apostle Paul refers to in the scripture text quoted at the top of the chapter, *2 Corinthians 3:17*. Notice the word used in John 8:31 to describe the application in which freedom is received: **abide.**

Liberty is not gained in Christian dialogue, simply reading spiritual quotes or commentary, nor is it found in the revelation or anointing of others, or in our church affiliation. **Liberty – Freedom – Discerning God's Truth is only accessible once we've accepted and therefore *submitted* to the Word of God.** When we submit to God, we will know the truth and the truth will set us free; we will cultivate liberty—our minds will be set free, regardless of what we've experienced and regardless of our current circumstance.

We are shown this example of freedom from psychological bondage in the life of Joseph in the book of Genesis.

After a host of seemingly negative experiences:

- Joseph was sold into slavery by his brothers

- He was falsely accused of pursuing adulterous relationship with his master's wife, resulting in his imprisonment

- He served two years in prison for a crime he did not commit, after he already served an extended period of time enslaved under an Egyptian guard

Through it all, Joseph had integrity: the ability to hold fast to the promises of God while being longsuffering and faithful; Joseph was a believer.

The Bible proclaims that **we have the same spirit of faith** (2 Corinthians 4:13). Therefore, do not lose heart. Even though our outward man is perishing, yet the inward man is being renewed day by day. For our light affliction, which is but **for a moment**, is working for us a far more exceeding and eternal weight of glory (2 Corinthians 4). This means that, by the power of the Holy Spirit, we have access to the same spirit of faith which was in Paul, the same spirit of faith which was in Joseph, the same spirit of faith which was in Job as well as other biblical writers, prophets, apostles and disciples. But, most importantly, the same spirit of faith which was in Christ Jesus is in you and me! We simply must activate it.

God is continually stretching our character. A season of despair, lack, suffering or longing prepares us for greatness, discipline, and growth. Don't allow your past or current circumstance to keep you in bondage. Instead, abide in His word and accept the liberty that the Spirit of the LORD affirms.

Prayer

Dear Heavenly Father, Faithful and Loving One; continue to prune the spirit of Your people so we may produce the fruit of the Spirit. May we be continually fulfilled in You.

Chapter 6

———————•———————

Back to the Altar

"When an unclean spirit goes out of a man, he goes through dry places, seeking rest; and finding none, he says, 'I will return to my house from which I came.' And when he comes, he finds it swept and put in order. Then he goes and takes with him seven other spirits more wicked than himself, and they enter and dwell there; and the last state of that man is worse than the first" (Luke 11:24-26).

Notice that in the book of Luke 11:24-26, **Jesus is documented speaking** in *generalized* **terms using the word, "man."** The book of Matthew also uses the same generalization when discussing the historical account of unclean spirits. **Jesus is very careful not to tie a label, title, or association to this "man."**

Jesus doesn't say, "when an unclean spirit goes out of a Christian;" He doesn't say, "when an unclean spirit goes out of a Jew;" He doesn't say, "when an unclean spirit goes out of the fornicator," or, "when an unclean spirit goes out of liar;" God doesn't say, "when an unclean spirit goes out of a sinner."

Jesus is intentionally and specifically generalizing the text —He does not want the hearer to think they are above reproach, that because we are in Christ, or battling that particular sin we aren't susceptible to this type of attack. For the Bible says, "All have sinned and fallen short of the glory of God (Romans 3:23)," that even a "righteous man may fall seven times… (Proverbs 24:16)."

Jesus is giving us a stern warning.

Notice, the Apostle Paul is noted saying in Romans 8:1, *"There is therefore now no condemnation to them which are in Christ Jesus who walk not after the flesh, but after the Spirit."* Condemnation is usually defined in one of two ways: The expression of very strong and definite criticism. Or, the action of condemning someone to punishment; sentencing.

In Romans 8:1, Paul is referring to the latter.

As noted in the scripture above, we're only protected **when we walk in the Spirit**, not in the flesh. This means that we are *all* accessible to the level of attack described in Luke 11:24-26, as we all are fleshly beings. Therefore, we have a great responsibility to guard our souls. Anytime a believer moves according to the flesh: commits adultery, engages in fornication, values anything above God (career, money, material possessions, or relationships), is envious or jealous, gossips or complains (see Galatians 5:19-21), they are **not covered** by the Spirit and they open themselves up to greater attack. **Our walk therefore becomes more difficult because we have weakened our spiritual immune system.**

Additionally, the book of Job serves as a reminder that the strength of our relationship with God doesn't prevent us from persecution, attacks, or trials; in fact, we learn throughout scripture that it is in obedience to Christ which makes us a target and sometimes in God's eyes, a candidate for persecution! Jesus, not Paul; Jesus, not Timothy; Jesus, not Luke, but JESUS declares, "Behold, I send you out in the midst of wolves. Therefore be wise as serpents and harmless as doves" (Matthew 10:16). Though Jesus was speaking directly to the disciples, like most of scripture, this applies to us also! Jesus sends out in the midst of wolves, commands that we are wise as serpents and harmless as doves.

In the book of Job, in both verses 1:8 and 2:3, a very popular but often easily forgotten part of scripture, God is recorded asking Satan—the liar, the accuser—"Have you considered My servant Job, that there is none like him on earth, a blameless, and upright man, one who fears God and shuns evil?"

The issue many of us have been faced with at one time or another is our ability to be affirmed through faith in Christ as we are persecuted or tested. In most cases, God is simply allowing our faith to develop and mature.

It is time to lay out before Jesus. Tell Him your struggles and ask Him for strength! Be still and allow Jesus to not only lead you, but also cleanse you completely.

Because **Luke 11:24-26** is so powerful yet continually overlooked, I have broken down each verse for your spiritual consideration:

Luke 11: 24-26

Verse 24. *"When an unclean spirit goes out of a man, he goes through dry places, seeking rest; and finding none, he says, 'I will return to my house from which I came.'*

When Jesus delivers us, the unclean spirit or spirits are not yet cast into hell at that moment. They begin roaming around the earth seeking unprepared souls. The reference to dry places in this text means barren: unproductive, unfruitful.

The unclean spirit is seeking a soul that lacks vision.

Unclean spirits are weak. They're cowards. Sometimes, instead of trying to find rest in a soul with a purpose, one that aligns their life with Christ, they will return to a place of comfort: a barren soul. What Jesus is basically saying is the unclean spirit felt so comfortable that he called the soul home – even after he left.

Just because we have been delivered doesn't mean we have been completely cleansed and it doesn't mean we are whole. Sometimes the unclean spirits that we are up against require spiritual warfare: fasting, prayer, and discipline!

Verse 25. *"And when he comes, he finds it swept and put in order."*

Your Bibles may say, "swept and garnished."

Instead of the unclean spirit coming back to a place that is reflective of the wholeness of Christ (a righteous, obedient, holy soul), he finds it empty. There are many times we have been delivered, but end up battling the same issues because we haven't secured our relationship with Jesus. Therefore, we leave the door open for greater attacks.

Verse 26. *Our last scripture reads, "Then he goes and takes with him seven other spirits more wicked than himself, and they enter and dwell there; and the last state of that man is worse than the first."*

There are 3 points to be made here:

1. Again, believers must not only seek to be continually delivered from sin, but also to align ourselves in complete obedience to the Holy Spirit submission to the word of Jesus, as well as continual and fervent prayer. The Apostle Paul said it this way: "I die daily" (1 Corinthians 15:31).

2. Unclean spirits are united against believers. For us to stand against them, we too, as believers in Christ, must also be united. We must support

our brothers and sisters in the Faith and create healthy, edifying relationships with other believers.

3. If we're not completely rooted in a relationship with Jesus, if we don't subject every component of our life over to Jesus, if we haven't changed the content of our heart, then we open ourselves up to greater struggles and attacks. Jesus says it this way in John 5:14, "Sin no more, lest a worse thing come upon you."

We must not only close every door to sin, but also change our hearts. We must remain steadfast in the faith. Return to the altar and submit yourself unto the LORD our God!

Prayer

Dear Heavenly Father, Merciful and Gracious One; grant us discerning wisdom of Your Word, not looking or thinking about anyone else, but discerning Your will over our own lives. Help us, Father, to bind ourselves to You, so that through You, we may overcome every obstacles and endure our daily cross.

Chapter 7

———•———

You Haven't Suffered Yet

*"Only let your conduct be worthy of the gospel of Christ, so that whether I come and see you or am absent, I may hear of your affairs, that you stand fast in one spirit, with one mind—striving together for the faith of the gospel, and not in any way terrified by your adversaries, which is to them a proof of perdition, but to you of salvation, and that from God. For to you it has been granted on behalf of Christ, not only to believe in Him, **but** also to suffer for His sake" (1 Philippians 1:27-29).*

Beloved, an authentic conversion experience in which you're called by Christ in any capacity—produces transformation.

If you confess with your mouth that Jesus is Lord and believe in your heart that God saved Him from the dead, the Bible says you shall be saved (Romans 10:9). **However**, that text is qualified by righteousness. Romans continues, "For with the heart a person believes, resulting in righteousness, and with the mouth he confesses, resulting in salvation" (Romans 10:10). Galatians 2:16 says, "Knowing that a man is not justified by the works of the law, but by the faith of Jesus Christ."

Simply stated, our behavior is a reflection of our belief system. It is the moral compass Jesus uses to not only to identify, but also ultimately judge our character.

If your life in Christ remains **predominantly** the same as it was before you seemingly came to Christ, you have not been "converted." You had an emotional experience. Anytime decisions are based solely out of **our** emotions, we are not mentally prepared to bear the burden of discipleship. An authentic conversion encounter produces *revelation* and *transformation*, not simply emotional response.

Jesus said, "Assuredly, I say to you unless you are converted and become as little children, you will by no means enter the kingdom of heaven" (Matthew 18:3). Another words, unless you become pliable, humble, and teachable, you will not enter the kingdom of heaven. Often times, believers love to hear and speak about the privileges and glory of the Kingdom. Seldom do we ever acknowledge the character, virtue and the depth of humility required.

In the Bible, Jesus reveals the depth of TRANSFORMATION He **requires** from His followers, His Church, by calling over a little child, and setting the child in the mist of His disciples. A child that has not yet been exposed to the elements of the culture in which we live in, **naturally** does not desire authority.

They **are** teachable, humble, loving, and **willingly dependent** on their parents. Jesus says to His disciples, those who left their businesses, who left their families, who sacrificed their relationships to follow Him, "unless you are converted and become as little children, you will by no means enter the kingdom of heaven" (Matthew 18:3).

We live in a society that has glamourized sin: lust, greed, materialism, fornication, anger, pride. Christianity has accepted and adapted to a lifestyle of self-indulgence, vanity, gossip, lewdness and complaining. Many have come to Christ, but haven't been transformed, still holding on to the worldly way of living, consumed by their emotions and circumstances. Some of you may have changed a couple of things, but you haven't been *transformed*. Your mind has not been renewed. Instead of becoming one with Christ, many believers are embracing a demonic culture: lust, greed, anger, pride, vanity, lewdness and self-indulgence.

In the book of Philippians, through a vision, God called the Apostle Paul to preach the gospel in Macedonia during his second missionary journey. As a result, the first church in Europe was established in Philippi.

The Apostle Paul wrote the Epistle to the Philippians to rejuvenate the spiritual discipline of all the saints—the church, with the bishops, the overseers, and deacons— which literally meant servants. Paul was in chains. He was beaten, mocked, and delivered as a prisoner from Jerusalem into the hands of the Roman Empire.

In prison, Apostle Paul's prayer was "that the church would abound in love, more and more in knowledge and all discernment. That you may approve the things that are excellent, that you may be sincere and without offense till the day of Christ, being filled with the fruits of righteousness which are by Jesus Christ to the glory and praise of God" (Philippians 1:9-11).

Paul's faith in Jesus, his love for the brethren, his commitment to discipleship and the growth of the church was not predicated on his circumstance or his emotions. The Apostle Paul **understood that building God's kingdom was not only about believing in Christ but also suffering for His sake.**

The reason so many of us are struggling in our Christian walk is because we have no spiritual roots.

The foundation—the platform in which most modern-day believers operate—is fixated on temporal affairs. It's fixated on our emotions and our circumstance, manipulating and separating scripture from its context to appease the flesh. Seldomly seeking the **truth** of the One we confess to believe in; Jesus Christ.

Seldomly seeking the truth of the One we proclaim to put our trust in—being confident of this very thing, that He which has begun a good work in you will perform it until the day of Christ Jesus (Philippians 1:6).

Alexander Crummell, an American scholar, minister, and the founder of the American Negro Academy, the first major learned society for black Americans said, "It is a sad reflection that a sense of responsibility (in the gospel) which comes with **power** is the rarest of things."

The Apostle Paul's mandate was more than a call for repentance—it was an indictment on the church. It was a formal charge to be likeminded, having the same level of love, *being* of one accord, not with the world, but **one with Christ**.

The book of Philippians captures the four premises of the believer, which is the baseline for Christianity: Life in Christ. "Baseline" is simply defined as a starting point. The four premises of Christ-like character is to:

1. Glorify Christ

2. Be Like Christ

3. Gain Christ

4. Be Content in Christ

Our mandate for living as Christians is to glorify Christ, be like Christ, gain Christ, and be content in Christ.

Someone is saying, "Well, Minister Angela, how do I do that?"

"Only let your conduct be worthy of the gospel of Christ" (Philippians 1:27).

"Let no corrupt word proceed out of your mouth, but what is necessary for edification, that it may impart grace to the hearers… (Ephesians 4:28).

Let all bitterness, wrath, anger and evil speaking be put away from you, with all malice. (Ephesians 4:31)

Be kind to one another, tenderhearted, forgiving one another, even as God in Christ forgave you. (Ephesians 4:32)

We are called to *Be Like Christ*

"Standing fast in one spirit, with one mind - striving together for the faith of the gospel" (Philippians 1:27).

What does that mean?

Love your enemies. Show them kind and sincere affection.

Bless those who curse you, and do good to those who hate you (Luke 6:28).

Bless, bless, bless! Do not gossip or complain about, get annoyed with, become disrespectful towards, but *bless* those who curse you!

Blessing is defined as pronouncing words in a spiritual manner, to invoke divine favor upon someone.

Jesus said it this way, "Father, forgive them for they know not what they do (Luke 23:43)!"

One important way the Bible commands for us to be like Christ is "Give to everyone who asks of you. And from him who takes away your goods, do not ask for them back" (Luke 6:30).

The Bible instructs us to *Gain Christ*

We must seek wisdom and understanding.

We must draw from and imitate who Jesus is: loving, compassionate, peaceful, patient, kind, longsuffering, gentle, faithful, temperate, and forgiving.

Spiritual maturity is tied to obedience, not time.

Half of the New Testament is about being *Content in Christ*

This not only means believing in Jesus, but also suffering for His sake. "If you suffer with Him, you will reign with Him. If you suffer for Him, you will rule with Him. If **we** deny Him, He also will deny **us**" (2 Timothy 2:12).

But, the good news is, **"AFTER you have suffered for a little while, the God of all grace, who called you to His eternal glory in Christ, will Himself perfect, confirm, strengthen and establish you" (1 Peter 5:10).**

Jesus is perfecting you. Jesus is confirming you. Jesus is strengthening and establishing you. Trust Him. His ways are not like our ways, nor His thoughts like our thoughts! "There is a way *that seems* right to a man, but its end is the way of death" (Proverbs 14:12).

Prayer

Dear LORD, not our will, but let Thine will be done! In Jesus name.

Chapter 8

———— • ————

Our Heavenly Father Determines Who We Become

"But you are a chosen generation, a royal priesthood, a holy nation, His own special people, that you may proclaim the praises of Him who called you out of darkness into His marvelous light"
(1 Peter 2:9).

In this chapter, we will be taking a look at the genealogy of Jesus Christ. You will find this is **not a glorious genealogy filled solely** with honor, but much like me and my family, and much like many of you and your families, **the bloodline of Jesus Christ is penetrated with scandal and disgrace.**

For your clear understanding, I will be quoting from the English Standard Version (notes added by the author for clarification and thoughtful consideration):

(READ SLOW)

The Gospel According to Matthew, Chapter 1:1-11, 16

Verse 1 "The book of the genealogy of Jesus Christ, the son of David, the son of Abraham.

² Abraham (*who received promise in his old age*) was the father of Isaac, and Isaac the father of Jacob (*who had 4 wives*), and Jacob the father of Judah and his brothers (*who sold Joseph into slavery*),

³ and Judah the father of Pherez and Zerah by Tamar (*a woman of scandals repute*), and Pherrez the father of Hizron, and Hizron the father of Ram,

⁴ and Ram the father of Amminadab, and Amminadab the father of Nashon, and Nashon the father of Salmon,

⁵ and Sal-mon the father of Boaz by Rahab (*Rehab who was a Canaanite harlot from Jericho*), and Boaz the father of Obed by Ruth (*a Moabite woman – Ruth was a descendant from an incestuous relationship*), and Obed the father of Jesse, (*who overlooked and did not consider his younger son to be worthy of leadership*)

⁶ and Jesse the father of David the king (*a murder who had an adulterous affair, nevertheless, because the sincerity of his repentance and worship, declared by the Lord, a man after His own heart*)

And David was the father of Solomon by the wife of Uriah (*the writer of the book of Matthew was so offended by Bathsheba and how she dishonored her husband, that he refused to call her by her name, but simply states that she is the wife of Uriah*),

[7] and Solomon the father of Rehoboam, and Rehoboam (*who worshiped idolatry*) the father of Abiya (*who names means my Father is God*), and Abiya the father of Asphr (*a skilled singer and poet who worshiped God*),

[8] and Asphr the father of Jehoshaphat (*known as a zealous follower of the commandments of God*), and Jehoshaphat the father of Jo-ram (*who embraced false prophets*),

and Joram the father of Izziah (*who became Judah's eleventh king at age 16, and held the second longest tenure as Judah's monarchy, 52-years*).

[9] and Izziah the father of Jotham, and Jotham the father of Ahaz, and Ahaz (*a weak and idolatrous king*) the father of Hizekiah, (*the son of a godless father who did what was* **good** *and* **right** *and* **faithful** *before the LORD*).

[10] and Hizekiah the father of Manasseh, and Manasseh (*who erected idolatry*) the father of Amos, and Amos (*a humble shepherd called to be a Prophet by God to deliver a stern warning of the judgement that was upon the people of Israel*) the father of Josiah,

Verse 11 and Josiah the father of Jechoniah and his brothers, at the time of the deportation to Babylon.

I would like to pause right there for a moment. I'm going to ask you to do something that, for a number of you, will be extremely uncomfortable. Close your eyes and think about your paternal father. If you know nothing about your biological father, think of the man who raised you. If you were not raised by any man, think about the pain you have carried and the impact of not having a father has had on you.

Take this moment to ponder the above as well as what you have read.

Now, let's skip down to Matthew 1:16.

[16] and Jacob the father of Joseph the husband of Mary, of whom Jesus was born, who is called Christ.

Before you continue to read, I need you to close your eyes one more time and say to yourself, "Jesus, knows me."

According to famed psychiatrist, Aaron Temkin Beck, regarded as the father of cognitive theories describes the following: "Cognitive Behavioral Therapy, which is commonly used to treat disorders like depression, phobias, anxiety, and addiction, is a form of psycho-therapeutic treatment that focuses on changing negative behavior by altering the influential thoughts and feelings an individual has."

The Bible simply says it this way: "For as a man thinks in his heart, so is he" (Proverbs 23:7).

Cognitive Behavioral Therapy as noted by Mr. Beck, is believed to be thoughts and feelings that influence and reinforce the behavior of a person. For example, if someone thinks negatively about their self-image and abilities, he or she will have low self-esteem and, as a result, he or she may avoid social situations or miss out on advancement and growth opportunities.

By changing the thought patterns of an individual, his or her behavior will also change; a notion that is derived from several biblical principles and New Testament teaches, though it may not be directly accredited as such, similar to much of modern psychological "discoveries".

Let me make it clear for you:

> The moment you think you're intelligent, you will behave intelligently.

> The moment you believe in the power of prayer, you will pray.

> The moment you accept God has purposed you to be a spouse, you will break off casual relationships.

> The moment you believe that whatsoever you sow you will reap, you will give, encourage, and support others.

As noted in the scripture overview for this chapter, it doesn't matter where you come from, it matters what you think. Let me, again, prove it to you:

Ahaz (*a weak and unsuccessful king who worship idolatry: rejected God and worshiped pagan images*) was the father of Hezekiah, (*a king that the Bible calls the son of a godless father who did what was* **good** *and* **right** *and* **faithful** *before the*

LORD his God – during his tenure, Hezekiah purged the people of Judah and established the rightful order of worship)…

and Hezekiah was the father of Manasseh, (*who erected idolatry*) was the father of Amos (*a humble shepherd called to be a Prophet by God*). Matthew 1:9 -10

It doesn't matter where you come from, it matters what you think.

The genealogy of Jesus Christ reveals that who our biological father is, is completely irrelevant; it is our thoughts, cultivated through our relationship with Jesus that declares who we become.

My biological father had three children by three different women and has done some horrible things in his past. He was never actively engaged in my childhood or early adulthood. But that isn't going to stop me from pursuing and answering the call of ministry that God has placed over my life. And, it will not hinder my thoughts on marriage, families or relationships. I forgive my biological father, I love my biological father, and I seek to honor and serve him. *I decided* not to allow his actions to influence how I operate.

The fact that I didn't have a relationship with my biological father growing up, hasn't stopped me from writing books, excelling in my personal goals, or pursuing Jesus. At one time it did. I felt unloved, forgotten, and ashamed. BUT I changed my mind!!! I decide to believe that I am a daughter of the most High God, an heir to the Kingdom!

Who our father is **or** is not may challenge us emotionally, it may challenge us psychologically, and it may even challenge us physically, but through Jesus Christ we have the power to overcome any obstacle by changing how we think.

Your *faith* dictates your experience, not your *circumstance*.

The issue for many of us is not our upbringing; it is that we choose not to be accountable for our thoughts or actions. We have yet to learn how to "take captive every thought to make it obedient to Christ" (2 Corinthians 10:5).

As both the Bible and cognitive behavioral therapy point out, our thoughts effect our emotions, how we think, how we feel, how we act and how we relate to other people.

The Bible says, "If you are willing and obedient you will eat the good things of the land" (Isaiah 1:19).

For many of us, it's not our father, and it's not our circumstance that hinders us. It's that we are not *willing* and we are not *obedient* to become disciplined followers of Christ.

Let me say this again: the problem with many is not our father and is not our circumstance. It's that we are not *willing* and we are not *obedient* to be transformed by the renewing of our mind!

Jesus came through 42 generations of abuse, harlotry, lust, broken marriages, neglect, violence, rape, murder, abandonment, prostitution, idolatry, and incest. And yet, through all that, the power of Christ was able to release forgiveness, self-control, humility, repentance, faithfulness, joy, kindness, obedience, hope and love to those who worship and submitted to God.

According to cognitive behavior therapy and the Bible, one must change a negative thought process in order to change a negative behavior (Romans 12:1-2). According to the book PSYCH101, *Cognitive Distortion* can be ascribed in ten components. I am going to review seven.

1. **Overgeneralization:** Using an isolated situation and broadly assuming all others are the same way.

   a) **Example One:** Your father abandoned your mother, so you assume marriage isn't valuable. You assume that if you were to get married, it would end in divorce.

   b) **Example Two:** The last person you confided in hurt and lied to you, so you assume that anyone else you confide in will hurt and lie to you, too.

2. **All-or-nothing thinking:** Thinking in terms of absolutes and are thus unable to compromise is a cognitive distortion.

3. **Emotional reasoning:** Instead of looking at a situation objectively by studying the facts

(spiritual truths), you let your emotions govern your thoughts concerning the situation.

    a) For example: You take a flight to visit someone in another state. During the flight, you experience a significant amount of turbulence. After your trip, you decide to never fly again.

4. **Jumping to conclusions:** Assuming the worst even when there is not sufficient evidence to back that assumption.

5. **Mental Filter:** Overlooking positive events that occurred in your life and mentally singling out the bad events.

6. **Should statements:** If, instead of attempting to deal with how things currently are, you focus on how things should be, you suffer from cognitive distortion.

7. **Labeling and mislabeling:** Giving false and cruel labels to other people and to yourself.

    a) **Example One:** To someone who is direct, you label them as rude.

    b) **Example Two:** You're professional, educated, and confident in your call and divine assignment, yet you dummy down when people label you as stuck up.

If you fit into any of those categories, you suffer from *cognitive distortion*, a serious and real issue.

We must stop blaming our earthly father, our mother, our children, our spouse, our ex, our co-workers, our supervisors, our pastor and those in leadership. Beloved, it is time to be accountable for our behavior, which is reflective of our thoughts.

"Trust in the LORD with all thine heart; and lean not unto thine own understanding. In all thy ways acknowledge Him, and He shall direct thy paths" (Proverbs 3:5-6).

Prayer

Dear Jesus, thank You for being the perfect example of love, hope and faith! Help us dear God to live more abundantly in You.

Chapter 9

———————•———————

Examining, First Myself

"How many are my iniquities and sins? Make known to me my rebellion and my sin" (Job 13:23).

In my assignment as a prayer intercessor in my local church I was called upon to intercede on behalf of the congregation during noon day prayer. I was so humbled and truly honored that Jesus would trust me with such an important, sacred and powerful assignment. Initially, I was assigned to pray on Thursday's on behalf of our Mother's board. Truly I felt unworthy to pray for women whose faith has been tested, tried through fire and found true. I was so, so, so humbled and so amazed at this opportunity to serve. A few of months in, I was reassigned to Friday's prayer. Still humbled, and still grateful. But, that humility was coupled with confusion when no one would show up to noon day prayer on Friday's. And, I thought: "Jesus, the bible say's your gift will make room for you (Proverbs 18:16)... where are the people I'm supposed to be covering in prayer???" Of course, my assignment included praying for the Bishop and his family, the needs of the church and community, as well as the body of Christ and sinners alike; and I owned that with all humility, integrity and seriousness, but I still started to question God. And, I know God is not the author of confusion.

I kept asking... And, one day, Jesus answered me. Jesus reminded me how I used to cry out to Him constantly for an opportunity to worship Him alone in His sanctuary a year and a half ago prior. I used to almost beg my Pastor at that time for time alone in the church, but because I wasn't the Assistant Pastor, President of the Deacon Board, or I didn't work as part of the senior administrative staff, I was rarely afforded the opportunity. Members (including leadership) were only permitted in the sanctuary during certain times, and those times happen to be when several people were in close proximity. I understood protocol and the safety precautions in place because the church was in an underserved and high crime area. However, I longed to be with Jesus in His holy temple alone.

Yes, I have a prayer closet; yes, I believe my home is a sanctuary to an extent... But there is something special about the LORD'S temple. A place where many have been delivered, healed, set free and where oil stains from prayer service reside. The place where babies are consecrated, people are baptized by the Holy Ghost... where the shell of a person has lain while their loved ones celebrate their life... something so pure and beautiful about the LORD'S temple. THEN one day I came to the understanding that I was in the midst of an answered prayer and immediately my confusion turned to a deeper level of worship, praise and gratitude. My soul begin to cry out.

So many times we allow the enemy to distract us from understanding that we are standing in the midst of answered prayers! It may just look different than we imaged but it is no less an answered prayer.

I used to beg God for 15 minutes in His Holy temple of uninterrupted time. No one asking if I was OK, or talking to me, or reminding me what time the church is closing, or feeling the presence of someone staring at me... And, the LORD has given me hours to glorify Him and privately intercede on the behalf of others in His Holy temple... How amazing and loving is our Faithful Father... beyond our comprehension. Regardless if some shows up or I'm there alone, regardless of when, or if, this assignment comes to an end, I'm so honored that He chose me to commune with Him in such a sacred space.

May we continually humbly submit to what we do not understand.

Prayer

Dear Heavenly Farther, thank You for being faithful when I have been faithless! Thank You for answered prayers. LORD, call me to a higher level of dependency on You. In Jesus name I pray.

Examining, First Myself

Angela Crudupt

Titles by Angela Monique Crudupt

Sent by Jesus: The Father sent Jesus, and Jesus sent you

Blessed Is: A Devotion of Overlooked Biblical Truth

Examine First, Yourself: A Testament to Spiritual Accountability, Self-Reflection and Understanding

Follow Angela Crudupt on social media @angelacrudupt

Visit Angela Crudupt's website at www.AngelaCrudupt.com